SERVICE IN MINISTRY
By

Rahshenia M. Patrick

DEDICATION

This book is dedicated to Shirley Bowie, Dorothy Walker, Rachelle Evans and The Todd Women.

ABOUT THE AUTHOR

My Story…

2018

I remember God tugging at my spirit, and I was tired of being tired. I knew I was destined for much more in life. I knew I had a purpose, but what it was at that moment, I had no clue. What I was sure of is that I needed to be reconnected with the source! I remember praying, "God whatever you are doing, please do not do it without me." I prayed for grace and mercy. I told God, "if you allow me to make it to Sunday, I will rededicate my life to you." I am sure we all have had those moments and did not follow through on our end. Now, I knew that I could have easily called the church and had one of the ministers pray with me. However, for me, it was the walk that I needed to take once again. I wanted to be in his house and fully in His presence with other believers. I would also need some accountability partners; like-minded people to help me navigate through this journey.

Sunday came, and when the Pastor made the call, I took the walk. I knew, at that moment, I needed to do something different to get different results. What do I mean by that? I was brought up in church. Accepted Christ as a little girl. As I became an adult and lived on my own, I continued to go to church here and there. It was all out of routine but no real connection. This time my soul needed more! I wanted to experience God on levels I never did before. I wanted to fully submit to his will for my life. Most importantly, I wanted to do it while I was in the right state of mind and not on my death bed begging God to spare my life.

The only way to do so for me was to get involved. I knew showing up every Sunday and going to Bible study would not be enough to keep me consistent. God sent someone in the church to confirm that I needed to get involved. I then started asking myself, Shenia, what are you good at?

Which ministry could you add value to? After taking some time to answer those questions and praying, I knew I loved making people feel welcome. I loved smiling. I enjoyed talking with people. I have a passion for tending to the needs of others. I loved jumping in and giving a helping hand.

Although extremely nervous, I joined hospitality. I was nervous because it was all new, but I could not allow fear to stop me. I knew I would not quit because one thing about me is when I say I am going to do something, I am all in. I tell my 2 sons all the time that when you start something you cannot quit in the middle. You have to finish strong. In the end, you reevaluate and have the option to continue on for the next season or move on to something else. So, mommy has to practice what she preaches unless the holy spirit says otherwise!

Within 2 months of being on hospitality, our current leader was ready to pass the baton. I remember us standing in the hallway as she mentioned it. One of the other members gently rubbed me on my back and said, "that's you". Screaming on the inside my flesh said, "no way!" The Holy Spirit confirmed at that moment it was me too. However, I told myself I am just supposed to be here and committed. I am doing my part. I do not need more or a title. I am just fine with what God has me currently doing.

2019…Fast forward to a few months later. Some things did not go as planned, and I knew then I needed to accept the call and say YES! God has a unique way of making things happen according to his will for our life. I laughed to myself and said, "Ok God, have your way". So, I transitioned into the leadership role, rather quickly. There was no time anymore to question, "why me or why not someone else?"

During this time, our Pastor was heavily involved in the community, and the church always had events. Anytime we are dealing with people, we must remind ourselves not all are saved, and even the saved fall short, including me. So, there were many encounters when dealing with God's children that I had to be stern but show love. My role was a reminder that I needed to allow others to see God's light and strive to win those who are lost.

I also had to learn rather quickly balancing ministry, family, and my work life! Being a wife and a mom of two boys, I always had my hands full. I resigned from a full-time job to pursue full time entrepreneurship. There were days I was forgetting about appointments or meetings I had in my personal life. The boys always had activities or field trips that they were used to me attending. As a wife, I also had to make sure my husband's needs were being met as well. I am not just talking about sexually, I had to make sure that home was taken care of while serving.

How can you feed the homeless, and you have not fed your family? God requires us to take care of the gifts he gives us. Some will ask, am I supposed to put the needs of my husband or children before ministry? The answer to that is simply no. We have to make good use of the time that we have. Yes, many days it seems easier said than done. God did not intend for us to do this thing called "life" alone. In ministry, you are not alone. So instead of trying to do it all yourself, delegate when necessary, especially when there are enough people to do so. You are not the only leader within the ministry you are involved in. You are assigned to pull out what God has already placed on the inside of them.

When it came to my business. I was able to have complete control of my schedule. I made a commitment to no longer work on Sundays or Wednesdays when we had church and Bible study. When I would get dates that we needed to serve, I would block the day immediately. I also stopped opening up my calendar so far in advance. Leaving room for me to be flexible. I learned it is okay to reschedule certain things or say I will not make it, especially when it did not serve any purpose.

Now, let us fast forward to the year 2020: the year God said He is requiring us all to be still. Covid-19 caused a lot of anxiety, grief, disconnection, and so much more for many people. The doors of the church were closed! I thank God for the knowledge he provided our Pastor with to allow service virtually. Our Pastor was so concerned about us still being plugged in that he set days aside each week at a set time for us to gather in groups according to certain ages.

Out of obedience, I did what was asked. Every Tuesday at 6:30pm, I was present on the line. I knew, for me, this was not a time to disconnect. We had no clue how long the doors of the church would be closed. I needed to remain fed, and because we are the church, the gospel needed to still be shared. Before the year was over, I got a call from my Pastor saying, I was one of the people God brought to his mind to facilitate our growth group.

Let me be honest, I said yes, of course. However, that nervous feeling came back! I was about to do something new once again. I felt like I had a good handle on hospitality, and that was my lane. Now God, you want me to teach and to women who are older than me? There were days I felt unqualified and did not know how I would get the task done. As I leaned more into him and not my own thoughts, I saw an increase in my faith. There would be days I was speaking, and I could feel the Holy Spirit take over. Many times, when I would study, He would give me questions to ask and examples to use. Even in those moments, I felt unqualified, but I continued to show up and did the work I needed to do behind the scenes. Feeling unqualified was personal and was the proof that I needed more time with God.

God had been preparing me to teach years before I ever knew I would. The job I resigned from; I was a facilitator for high-risk African American women. Later I transitioned to facilitating youth. This is all a reminder of Jeremiah 29:11. "For I know the plans I have for you," declares the Lord, "plans to prosper you and not to harm you, plans to give you hope and a future."

I find myself sitting a lot and just reflecting on all the things that God had done to prepare me for these various moments. He knew when I accepted the call that I would be nervous and feel unqualified. I would also experience a disconnection with him due to life's situations. Most importantly, God knows our genetic makeup. So, he knows our thoughts before we think them and our actions before we act them out. All I needed to do was have faith, trust, and believe in him to help me fulfill my purpose.

The Process…

I gave you a snippet of what my journey was like. However, I want you to understand there is an inevitable process for us! Walking with Christ is not always easy, but it is worth it!

There were so many days that I did not understand what was happening. I remember asking God to "make it make sense". God was pulling me out of my comfort zone. I had many moments when I needed to be still. I needed to silence the noise around me to hear God clearly. In that alone time, God would tell me there are some places I am taking you that I have to prepare you for. There are some people I need you to let go of. There are some things I need you to be watchful for. There is some work I need to do within you. I need you to trust me.

Oftentimes, these moments are very uncomfortable. You feel as if you are changing. Others make you feel like you are switching up or acting differently. When all along they are growing pains. You are growing, and you are evolving. It is time to let go of things that no longer fit and relationships that serve no purpose. Anything that is blocking you from fulfilling God's will for your life has to fall off. The shedding of anything unneeded is painful but necessary! There are days when you feel alone, days when you want to quit because it is easier to throw in the towel, and that's just what the enemy wants. They are all distractions to get you to compromise your reward.

Let me remind you God walks with you every step of life. He will strategically and intentionally send trusted individuals to remind you of things He has already confirmed for you. Remove the mask and allow yourself to be vulnerable with those individuals. These are the people who see you. Not the outer image of you but internally. They are there to walk beside you and are willing to intercede on your behalf. God never intended for us to do life alone. Therefore, it is important to stay connected with your brothers and sisters in Christ. The enemy will have your mind running rampant and isolating yourself.

I had to learn to shift my way of thinking. When people tell me that I am changing, I would remind myself I am not changing, I am becoming! You will outgrow people, and that is okay. Things you once loved doing with people you once loved to be with you may no longer have the desire.

I had to remind myself in those moments that they were connected to a version of me that has expired. So, it is not that I think I am better or judging their lifestyle. My soul desired more! When I wanted to do certain things or go certain places God said, "you do not belong there." I used to feel like an outsider when hanging out with old friends. I knew I was different and not in an arrogant or cocky way. It took me some time to fully realize that I was never supposed to fit in. I was set apart, and the more I tried to fit in, God made me uncomfortable. I had to keep pushing without looking back. You do not have solid faith unless it has been rocked.

During those times of uncertainty, unbelief and doubt are when you must seek your father's face and sit in his presence. When talking to God, I like to shoot it straight. God knows his daughter, and He knows I like to ask a lot of questions. Then there are some days I do not have the words to say. God loves us so much that even in those moments, the Holy Spirit intercedes on our behalf and prays that His will, will be done (Romans 8:26-27). God knows exactly how to respond back to us on a level that we can understand. He is just waiting on you to invite him to be in a relationship with him. My Pastor always says, "God is a gentleman". God will not force Himself on you. There will be many moments when He is speaking to you. It is up to you to respond. What are you waiting on to answer the call?

I challenge you, yes you, reading this. What is it that you are supposed to be doing? God has already revealed it to you, and someone has given you confirmation. So, get to it! God does not see us how we see ourselves. Everything we need is already in us! We just have to say YES.

I can tell you from my own experience God has already aligned the ministry and vision just for you. He has assigned everyone required to get you to your destination. He is just waiting on you.

My story is still being written and will be ongoing until my purpose is fulfilled on earth. In the meantime, what is your story? How many lives can be impacted behind you sharing it or walking in your purpose?!

Let us take some time together to walk through what Serving in Ministry Is. Keep in mind the process is different for each of us. There may be similarities, but they are different at core. The goal, however, is the same! To wholeheartedly serve our father!

Let's get started……

Table of Contents

Dedication.. 2

About The Author... 3

Introduction.. 16

Chapter ONE... 18

Why Are We Called to Serve?...................................... 18

Who Are We Called to Serve? Why?............................. 20

CHAPTER TWO.. 23

What Does it Mean to Serve in & Be A Part of a Ministry...23

CHAPTER THREE.. 26

Why is serving in The Church Important?..................... 26

CHAPTER FOUR... 29

Serving God Wholeheartedly..29

CHAPTER FIVE...34

What Does It Mean to Serve in The Church?.................34

CHAPTER SIX.. 37

Why is Serving God Important?.................................... 37

CHAPTER SEVEN... 43

How do you serve God by serving others?.................... 43

CHAPTER EIGHT... 47

Dealing with the Unsaved while serving 47

CHAPTER NINE 49

What Are the Blessings of Serving God? 49

CHAPTER TEN 53

Serving God in an Online Church 53

CHAPTER ELEVEN 59

What Are The Type of Ministries? 59

CHAPTER TWELVE 63

Being Comfortable with your ministry calling 63

CHAPTER THIRTEEN 65

Avoiding Burnout in Ministry 65

CHAPTER FOURTEEN 71

Setting Ministry Boundaries 71

CHAPTER FIFTEEN 74

Balancing Ministry and Family 74

Supporting Your Spouse Who is In Ministry 77

CHAPTER SIXTEEN 81

Managing Ministry Conflict 81

CHAPTER SEVENTEEN 87

Scriptures on Serving in Ministry 87-93

Servant in Ministry Commitment…………………………………… 94-96

INTRODUCTION

We exist as believers to fulfill three goals. That is to serve God, serve fellow believers, and serve others (mainly unbelievers).

These three mandates are broken into three groups. They are the up-reach, in-reach, and outreach.

Up-reach is our service to our maker. The one true God who has called us out of darkness into His marvelous light and has blessed us with so many wonderful gifts. We serve Him to thank Him for sending His only Son Jesus Christ, who left His glory in heaven and died for our sin, and as a result, redeemed us and saved us from the power and the consequence of our sin, which is death. U-preach is our worship, praise, and thanksgiving to Him.

In-reach, on the other hand, is all about our service to one another as believers in the church. It is perfectly exemplified by our Lord and Savior Jesus, who washed the feet of His disciples and commanded them to do the same in humility and service (John 13:1–17). God has empowered us with different gifts of the Holy Spirit to serve in the church to move the Kingdom of God forward. These gifts are given to us, not for our personal benefits alone, but for the church to teach, correct, bless, help, and inspire one another.

Finally, the Outreach. This is what the great commission was given to us by Jesus all about (Matthew 28:16-20). We are to go out and preach the gospel to the unsaved, baptize them and convert them into God's kingdom. This mission is very important because it deals with salvation, the soul of man, and where he will spend eternity. God does not want anyone to perish but to come to repentance. That is why we need to take this aspect of service seriously.

In this book, God will reveal to you everything you need to know about serving God, serving in the church, and dealing with unbelievers when serving. You learn about different ministries backed by the Word of God and how you can discover your calling and serve God effectively.

Everyone has been called to serve, and we have been promised both earthly and eternal blessings for our service to God and the church. As you open the pages of this book, open your mind to receive insight from God and open your ears to hear from Him.

If you have not discovered your calling, get ready to start because there is going to be a shift in your life. If you already have a ministry, your ministry is about to experience another level of growth.

Happy reading.

CHAPTER ONE

Why Are We Called to Serve?

The first reason why we are called to serve is that we are the children of God. We have been washed by the blood of Jesus, sanctified, and set apart. A sinner does not understand the concept of service or serving. This is because, in that state, man is full of pride and selfishness and cannot comprehend what it means to humble oneself to the service of another.

So, the first thing God does is to work on the heart of man and transform it by taking away the evil and darkness in it and replace them with love and light. At the point of salvation, the Bible in 2 Corinthians 5:17 says we become a new creature, with a new heart that can understand the ways and will of God such as service to God and man.

Secondly, we are called to service because we have been made vessels unto honor. We have been anointed for service and made vessels of honor, fit for the master's use, 2 Timothy 2:20-21. A sinful man cannot serve God and even if He tries to serve, his service will not be acceptable before God, because God cannot behold sin and the sacrifice of a sinner is an abomination unto God Habakkuk 1:13, Proverbs 15:8.

So, for us to become fit for the master's use, he makes us vessels unto honor by sanctifying and purifying us. When we are set apart, pure and holy, we are not only qualified to serve, but our service becomes acceptable to God and rewarding unto us. We have been empowered by God to serve.

Thirdly, we have been commanded to serve (John 13:17). Jesus served and did so because He loves us. Service is being selfless and putting the needs of others before your own. The meaning of Christianity is being like Christ. We are meant to be like Christ in every way (Romans 8:29) Since Christ served, we must serve.

We are called to reflect the love of Christ here on earth. People cannot see Christ, but they can see Christ in us. We give people the experience of Heaven here on earth through our service to God and humanity.

We are called to serve because the world is bleeding and in so much pain. The world needs healing and love. The world needs light because the darkness is getting thicker every day. We are the light of the world, and we carry the love of Christ in our hearts. The combination of these two powerful forces can save humanity and nations from the grip of the devil and bring salvation, peace, and joy.

We have been saved to save others. Called out of darkness to call others. We have been loved to love others and healed to heal others. Our shoulders should be the succor points for the downtrodden and depressed. Our presence should be an emblem of joy and relief to those suffering emotional, spiritual, and physical pain. We are to be like Christ who was always moved with compassion when he saw someone in need of help.

Who are we called to serve? Why?

As believers that are saved, washed, and sanctified, God has called us to serve in different capacities. Our service is not to ourselves but to God, fellow believers, and sinners.

Serve God

Serving God is not only when we go on a missionary journey to Africa or India, but our act of worship and how we live our lives to please Him. Service to God is living according to His and in obedience to His Word. Honoring Him and glorifying His name by our good deeds.

According to 1 Samuel 12:24, *Only fear the Lord and serve him faithfully with all your heart. For consider what great things he has done for you.* Two phrases stand out in this verse and they are instructive on the reason for our service to God and how we should serve Him.

The first is the last part of the verse which says we should consider the great thing God has done for us. What has God done for us? He sent His only Son Jesus Christ to die for our sins even before we were born. Jesus came for us and delivered us from the grave consequences of sin. When we consider this show of genuine love to us, we will willingly do anything to please God.

The second phrase tells us how to serve God for what He has done for us. It says, *"fear the Lord and serve him faithfully with all your heart."* Having considered what God has done for us, we must fear Him and serve Him faithfully and with the whole of our hearts. To fear God is not to run from Him but to reverence Him and acknowledge His sovereignty.

Serve Fellow Believers

In John 13:1-17 Jesus exemplified humility and what serving others means when He washed the feet of His disciples. Amazingly, the King of Kings and Lord of Lords went down on His knees to wash the dirty feet of ordinary everyday people.

What is also interesting is that after His deed He gave clear instructions to His disciples. In John 13:14, Jesus says, *If I then, your Lord and Teacher, have washed your feet, you also ought to wash one another's feet.* What Jesus is saying here is that we must serve one another. We must be humble and lend a helping hand to a brother or sister in Christ who is in need.

The Apostle Paul in his letter in Galatians 6:2 instructs us to carry one another's burdens. We do this by praying, encouraging, counseling, supporting, helping, and showing care to one another.

Serve Sinners

It doesn't make sense, right? Serving drug addicts, prostitutes, fornicators, alcoholics, murders, and all the worst sins we can think of. But come to think of it, we were once like that, and it was the service of others that brought us out of the wrong path to the right path.

Our service to sinners is to bring them out of darkness and bring them in contact with Jesus the light. In our daily living, let our lives preach unto others (Matthew 5:16.) We also serve them when we bind and lift the battered and broken and heal the sick. These are what Jesus commanded us to do in Matthew 28:16-20 and Mark 16:15-17.

Serving is not selective. Jesus washed the feet of Judas Iscariot even though He knew He would betray Him. When serving, we serve who needs to be served irrespective of who that person is. Service does not play favorites. We must emulate this and serve sinners irrespective of how sinful we think they are.

CHAPTER TWO

What Does It Mean to Serve in and Be A Part of A Ministry?

Service is not only restricted to ordained ministers or pastors but to everybody who is born of the water and the Spirit. We must understand that we do not have to be on the pulpit to serve in a ministry or be a part of a ministry.

Service is all-inclusive. We are all called to minister in different capacities according to our gifts (Romans 12:3-8.) We are parts of the Body of Christ, called to function at different capacities for the furtherance of the Gospel.

Serving in a ministry does not only mean serving in a church alone. Our service should not be restricted to a geographical location but reflect in every area of our lives, in all we do and wherever we find ourselves, and how we live our daily lives honoring and worshipping God and helping one another.

We must always remember that we are all called into ministry, and no matter the position we hold, we must minister and do what God expects of us. To serve in a ministry is to live our daily lives doing God's will and obeying Him. Serving the Lord should be our attitude and action and not necessarily filling a role in the church. Of course, serving God in the church is great and important as believers (we will get to that shortly); however, the ministry is not limited to that.

Here are some of the areas we can minister:

Ministry in Family

Parent, Child and Spouse are the main categories of ministries within the family we all fall into one or even all of them.

The home is one of the most important mission fields for parents. The role the family plays in the church and society at large is tremendous. Parenting is one of the biggest ministries endorsed by Jesus (Matthew 19:13-15.) Parents are already in full-time ministry, and their duties are to teach their children the ways of the Lord and ensure they do the right thing always (Proverbs 22:6, Ephesians 6:4.)

Likewise, as children, we are to respond to the ministry of our parents through obedience (Colossians 3:20, Proverbs 23:22.) We must obey our parents and the Word of God which they teach us daily. Obedience is an act of service to God because He commanded it.

Finally, as spouses, we are to serve each other in love and submission (Colossians 3:18-19.)

Serving God at Work

"Whatever you do, work heartily, as for the Lord and not for men, knowing that from the Lord you will receive the inheritance as your reward. You are serving the Lord Christ" (Colossians 3:23-24.)

The scripture above summarizes this segment on what it means to serve in and be a part of the Ministry. The Bible says here that whatever we do should be done as service to God and not men because it is from God our reward comes.

This verse should influence our attitude towards our 9-5 job and not our service in the Church alone. We should have the mindset that despite having a boss figure, who is our employer and hands us a paycheck, our services in our offices are unto God and not our boss and customers.

When we have this mindset, then we will do our work with diligence. We will give our best even when our supervisors are not on the ground because we know that the omnipresent supervisor is watching from above. We will be honest and not be involved in any shady deals. Serving and being a part of the ministry is living every aspect of our lives serving God and serving others

CHAPTER THREE

Why Is Serving in The Church Important?

To serve in the church is to be a part of those working to ensure that everything goes on successfully in the church service. Service in the church is service to God and man. When we serve in the church, we use our gifts and talents to worship God and do His work.

Serving in the church starts from the preacher who mounts the altar and holds the mic to the cleaner who washes the toilet and cleans the windows and seats of the church. Irrespective of the position we hold in the church and how significant or less significant we feel our services are, there are rewards for what we do, and God is the rewarder.

Also, we need to understand that there are no small or great services in the church; service is simply service.

As believers, we must know that we have not been called by God to warm the pews, sing and shout hallelujah! God has called us all to serve. So, we must find a way to serve God and serve others in the church.

Here is why serving in the church is important.

We Find Fulfilment in Obeying God: Jesus told His disciples to serve one another. Every Word of God is a command, and every action taken according to the Word is an act of obedience. Whenever we serve in the church, whether as a singer, instrumentalist, cleaner, usher, youth leader, etc. we are obeying God. There is a peace of mind and joy that we experience when we know we are working in the will of God. Service in the church is obedience.

We Become Sources of Blessings to Others: In the place of service, God uses us to bless others. We become a conduit of blessings and through our service, we touch lives. In serving as a singer, the presence of God can manifest powerfully when we sing. As youth leaders, God can use us to snatch young adults from bad and harmful habits. As counselors, we can minister peace and restore joy into the lives of those going through emotional and mental storms. The idea is, God can use our office of service to change and transform the lives of others.

Our Gifts and Talents Find Expression: Many believers have incredible skills, talents, and abilities. Where else can one use them if not in the house of God? God is the giver of these gifts and talents and it is amazing how the church has given a platform for so many people to express themselves in service to God and others. When we serve God, we enjoy the best reward more than any paycheck, accolades, or earthly rewards.

We Find Purpose: We find purpose and meaning when we put the needs of others above ours. When we invest our energy, time, and money into the lives of others, we discover our potentials and hidden talents. We become more aware of God's calling upon our lives, and the direction He wants us to go in serving him and in life in general. Many believers have discovered their true calling in the place of service. Through volunteering to feed the poor and needy in the community, some have gone ahead to open charity homes and NGOs pulling massive resources and blessing many lives.

CHAPTER FOUR

Serving God Wholeheartedly

And you shall love the Lord your God with all your heart, with all your soul, with your entire mind, and with all your strength.' This is the first commandment. - Mark 12:30

We are not promised to have a smooth and perfect ride in our journey of serving God. There will be times of difficulties. Times when the road will be bumpy. Times when we feel like turning back and take the seemingly easy path of being an ordinary church member who just attends service on Sunday mornings and warms the seat and zooms off as soon as the closing prayer is said.

Feeling this way is valid, and it is a part of our journey in service. However, our response and reaction during this phase will determine the state of our hearts towards our service. It will reveal if we are serving God just for the sake of getting busy or doing it with the understanding of what it means to serve. That is what separates those serving wholeheartedly and those serving just for the fun of it.

God expects us to serve Him wholeheartedly. But first, what does it mean to serve God wholeheartedly?

Before anything else, we must first love God. Without genuine love in our hearts, we cannot serve God as we ought to. Love is the first requirement for total service to God.

"And now, Israel, what does the Lord your God require of you, but to fear the Lord your God, to walk in all His ways and to love Him, to serve the Lord your God with all your heart and with all your soul" -Deuteronomy 10:12

To serve God with the whole of our hearts means:

To Serve Him in Spirit and in Truth

"But the hour is coming, and now is, when the true worshipers will worship the Father in spirit and truth; for the Father is seeking such to worship Him. God is Spirit, and those who worship Him must worship in spirit and truth." - John 4:23-24

This is serving God not with our flesh but with all sincerity of our hearts. To serve God wholeheartedly, we must be filled with the Holy Spirit because the flesh is weak (Matthew 26:41).

We cannot rely on our flesh to serve God; it will fail us (Isaiah 40:29, 2 Chronicles 32:8.) The flesh seeks pleasure and comfort. The flesh does not want stress. It is proud and does not want to submit to the leading of God and church leaders and to serve others. That is why we need the Holy Spirit.

It was the Holy Spirit working in Jesus that empowered Him to serve us to the point of death on the cross of Calvary. If we really want to give our all to serve, then we must lay aside our will and desires and surrender to God's will for our lives.

To Serve God Without Grumbling

"And above all things have fervent love for one another, for "love will cover a multitude of sins." Be hospitable to one another without grumbling. As each one has received a gift, minister it to one another, as good stewards of the manifold grace of God." - 1 Peter 4:8-10

Grumbling when serving God is as good as not serving at all. When we argue when we are asked to do something, we are allowing the devil to steal our blessings.

God wants people who will serve Him with a joyful heart. (Psalm 100:4). Grumbling while serving is a sign that you are forced to serve or do not want to serve. And if that is the case, it is better not to waste time and energy because such service would not be acceptable before God, and there would not be any blessings.

But when we serve wholeheartedly, we know that it is a rare privilege to be counted worthy to serve the King of all Kings. We will do His work with gladness, knowing that His blessings are innumerable.

To Serve God when No One is Watching

"...not with eyeservice, as men-pleasers, but as bondservants of Christ, doing the will of God from the heart" - Ephesians 6:6

When we do not do eye service or are not serving to please men, we are serving God Wholeheartedly. When we serve with the understanding that God is omnipotent and He is always beside us, we will do His work diligently. Service is an act of worship and not only about the physical activities we do. That is why the state of our hearts plays a key role in our work for God, not our intellect and muscle.

To serve God in the Face of Opposition.

"Who shall separate us from the love of Christ? Shall tribulation, or distress, or persecution, or famine, or nakedness, or peril, or sword?" - Romans 8:35
Oppositions will surely arise if we serve wholeheartedly, even from friends and family and people we love.

Job was facing a health challenge and financial crisis after losing all he had and fallen sick. His friends accused him, and even his beloved wife told him to curse God and die (Job 2:9). But Job refused. He held on even when he had no more reason to do so. He stayed with God all through and served him.

This should be our attitude towards service. When all those we know and love turn their backs on us and insult us because of our service to God, we should not look back but press on because when the blessings of serving come, they will wish they too had served.

Serving God in the face of opposition is difficult, but God is always there to give strength and grace to serve. One of the ways to know that our rewards are very close is how strong the opposition gets.

To Serve God When it is Not Convenient.

"Not lagging in diligence, fervent in spirit, serving the Lord" - Romans 12:11
Serving God when we do not feel like it and when our body seems weak and does not want to cooperate, but we still forge ahead, we are serving God wholeheartedly.

Sometimes we feel like wrapping ourselves in our warm blankets when it is cold and not going to church. Other times we just want to lay back, stretch our legs, and watch Netflix while snacking on some popcorn and drinks instead of sweating and expending energy in the place of service.

When we serve wholeheartedly, we say to ourselves what the apostle Paul said, *"But I discipline my body and bring it into subjection, lest, when I have preached to others, I myself should become disqualified."* - 1 Corinthians 9:27

To Serve God Even When It Does Not Make Sense

"Trust in the Lord with all your heart, And lean not on your own understanding; In all your ways acknowledge Him, And He shall direct your paths" - Proverbs 3:5-6

When it seems like there are no rewards for our service. When it seems like the people who are living reckless lives and not serving God are living better lives than us. When it seems we are laboring in vain, serving God wholeheartedly suggests we should hold on and not turn back. Sometimes, we will not get the point of our service, but we owe God and the people we serve the responsibility to remain focused and unwavering.

CHAPTER FIVE

What Does It Mean to Serve in The Church?

Serving in the church is a way of honoring God, worshiping Him, and doing His will.

Jesus has set the example of serving for us to follow throughout His life on earth. All that He did was in service to God and the Kingdom of God. Also, He served the people; the poor, the sick, the oppressed, the brokenhearted, and the needy. He also served His disciples, by teaching them, empowering them for service, and washing their feet. We learn from the life of Jesus that serving is of great significance, and God expects us to serve in different capacities and areas.

Serving in the local church is very good and goes a long way in terms of worship to God and service to people. However, serving should not be restricted to the four walls of the church. The works Jesus did were not only in the synagogue or chapels. Jesus utilized every opportunity and place He was to serve. He served in the field, in the boat, on the streets, in people's homes, etc.

Considering the life of Jesus, here are different ways we can serve in the local church.

Serving Inside the Church: As Christians, serving within the church is important. We serve during Sunday services, mid-week services, and other programs that are organized within the church. Serving in the church can be in different ways. There are many places we can choose to serve depending on our interests and skills. Some areas do not need skill.

Churches consist of different departments we can serve. We can serve as singers, greeters, ushers, camera handlers, slide controllers, graphic designers, cleaners, etc. The church is like a typical business organization, and almost all departments that exist there from finance to online are present in the church. So, any believer who is employed or self-employed can easily employ their skill-sets to serve in the church.

Serving Outside the Church: Serving within the church building might not be what everyone in the church can do because there are always people who sit and listen to the Word or get served by others. However, church activities are not restricted to Sunday services or other programs that take place within the church.

Christ has commanded us to go into the world, and the church today responds in different ways, like evangelism, outreaches, prison visitation, orphanage home ministry, and others. These are opportunities to serve. We can be a part of these mission duties by giving our time, money, and energy.

Serving God with Resources: the church is always in need of money to pay for missionary efforts, church events, building projects, and other projects in the church. Giving to meet these needs is an act of service and worship to God. Donations and offerings are good ways to serve God and contribute to Kingdom development.

God loves those that give to the work of His Kingdom "So let each one give as he purposes in his heart, not grudgingly or of necessity; for God loves a cheerful giver." (2 Corinthians 9:7)

CHAPTER SIX

Why Is Serving God Important?

We serve because we love God and it is a privilege to live for Him and His Kingdom because He died for us. What other way can we show our gratitude to God for sending His Son to die for our sins? What can we give Him who owns all things? How much can we pay He who has the cattle upon a thousand hills and made money come out from the mouth of a fish? The answer is nothing. The best way to worship God and thank Him for all He has done and all the things He is doing is for us to submit to Him for His use. We should count ourselves lucky and privileged to serve the Almighty God.

He Empowered us to Serve

Every Christian has at least one spiritual gift. God gave us these gifts to serve others and not for our personal use (1 Peter 4:10-11)

There are diversities of gifts, but the same Spirit. There are differences of ministries, but the same Lord. And there are diversities of activities, but it is the same God who works all in all. But the manifestation of the Spirit is given to each one for the profit of all: - 1 Corinthians 12:4 7.

These gifts include (1 Corinthians 12:7-11, Romans 12:6-8)

- A message of wisdom
- A message of knowledge
- Faith
- Healing
- Prophecy
- Distinguishing between spirits
- Speaking in different kinds of tongues
- The interpretation of tongues
- Serving
- Teaching
- Encouraging
- Giving
- Leading
- Showing Mercy

These gifts are given to us by the Holy Spirit basically to serve. When we use these gifts to serve others, we are serving God as well.

For example, many people need healing. When we minister healing to them, we are serving them and God at the same time. We lift them up from the sick by the power of God in us, and we obey God who has commanded us to go out and heal the sick (Matthew 10:8)

Many believers also need the wisdom to make decisions about different areas of their lives.

We Serve Him in Thanksgiving for the Gifts.

The best way to thank God for giving us His gifts is by serving Him with the gifts. We serve Him with these gifts by using them to expand His kingdom here on earth and depopulate the kingdom of Satan.

Consider it this way. How do you feel when someone you gave a little birthday gift responds by giving you a gift in exchange? You feel appreciated and happy, right? That is how our response to the gift God has so graciously given to us should be.

We do not deserve His gifts to us, but he still gave us. The best way to appreciate Him is to use these same gifts to serve Him. Our service to God is a little thank you gift to Him. When we do this, we should be ready for more.

We Serve God Because We Love Him

Our service to God is not as slaves but as Sons who have received adoption through the death of Jesus Christ. We are no longer condemned but saved and entitled to enjoy the inheritance of God. These inheritances are blessings.

We serve Him for His unconditional love towards us. Our service to Him is in worship, thanksgiving, and obedience to His Word. We serve God because that is one of the ways to prove our love for him and the people he has created.

What does the Bible say about serving?

The principle of serving in the Bible is the direct opposite to how it is viewed in the world. Serving in the kingdom of God is the opposite of serving in the kingdom of the world. How?
In God's kingdom, the kings serve the servants or the leaders serve the subjects, while in the world, servants serve kings.

First, the story of how Jesus washed the feet of His disciples paints a vivid picture of this principle of serving. Jesus, who is the master, teacher, king of kings, and the holy Son of God, went down on His knees with a towel around his waist and washed the feet of His disciples who were like servants and students to Him. He then wiped their feet clean with a piece of towel.

This single act of Jesus is like saying the president of the United States of America, taking off his expensive well-tailored suit, going down on his knees, and washing the dirty feet of the poor and homeless on the streets. That might be even extreme. Imagine him washing the feet of members of his cabinet/government. That sounds demeaning, right? But that is what we do in the Kingdom of God.

The Bible says we are kings (Peter 2:9, Revelation 1:6) All of us believers who have been washed by the blood of Jesus, are kings, but Jesus here is what Jesus instructed us to do in John 13:12-15 *"So when He had washed their feet, taken His garments, and sat down again, He said to them, "Do you know what I have done to you? You call Me Teacher and Lord, and you say well, for so I am. If I then, your Lord and Teacher, have washed your feet, you also ought to wash one another's feet. For I have given you an example, that you should do as I have done to you"*

Jesus is telling us believers, who are also kings to go down on our knees and wash one another's feet just as He did. Going down on our knees to serve shows humility. It means, it does not matter what our spiritual title or social status is, we will serve others. Serving others does not necessarily mean getting a bowl and water to wash someone's feet. But it could translate to helping the needy, the poor, and the people others will naturally run away from.

Serving according to the Bible also means using our gifts to serve others. It is all about putting the needs of others ahead of ours. Service is selflessness and not self-centered like it is practiced in the world; where people do everything for their own benefit.

As each one has received a gift, minister it to one another. - 1 Peter 4:10-11.

1 Peter 4:10-11 is instructive and clear about what our gifts should be used for. The primary goal of our service should not be to make money or for other selfish reasons. It is disheartening how many Christians today have made service in the church transactional. If they are not paid, they won't play the musical instrument or do any other thing they are skilled in.

The Book of Acts records how the members of the early church sold their lands, houses, and other valuable belongings and donated them to the apostles and shared them amongst the needy. That is the height of service, serving God with resources and gifts. But the reverse is the case in Churches today where professing believers insist on payment for service in the church. What an irony.

There is nothing wrong with the church appreciating the services of its servants with cash and other gifts out of love and not compulsion. But we need to know that our service is unto God whose reward is beyond anything a man can give and greater in multiple folds than any amount you can be paid. Collecting cash payment before serving the Lord is short-changing yourself.

CHAPTER SEVEN

How do you serve God by serving others?

The greatest commandment given to us by our Lord Jesus Christ is to love people as we love ourselves. Love cannot be complete without serving others. Love is more than a feeling; it is an action. If love is not demonstrated, then it is just a mere thought or confession. True love is backed by a series of consistent actions that confirm what we feel or profess.

To really show we love people, we must serve them, and in serving them, we are obeying God, and obedience to God is an act of service to Him.

Whatsoever we do to bless or help others, we are doing it unto God. *Then the King will say to those on His right hand, 'Come, you blessed of My Father, inherit the kingdom prepared for you from the foundation of the world: for I was hungry and you gave Me food; I was thirsty and you gave Me drink; I was a stranger and you took Me in; I was naked and you clothed Me; I was sick*

and you visited Me; I was in prison and you came to Me.'
(Matthew 25:34-36)

So, we must first have love in our hearts towards others so that we can easily serve them as we should. Here are some of the ways we can serve God by serving others.

Pay Your Tithes and Offerings

Tithes, offerings, and all other forms of donations are used for the furtherance of the kingdom of God. Funds for charitable efforts such as meeting the needs of the poor, orphans, widows, and others are obtained from our tithes and offerings. If we are faithful in giving, we are not only serving God, but we are also serving others by helping to take care of them.

Give to the Needy

One of the best ways to serve God by serving others is by giving. As common and cliché as giving sounds, it is a powerful way to serve people. People are always hungry and in need of shelter, clothing, and other basic human needs. When we serve the poor food and give them clean and good clothes, we are not only touching their lives, we are also serving God. *"Whoever is generous to the poor lends to the Lord, and he will repay him for his deed."*
- Proverbs 19:17.

Jesus was particular about the importance of doing all these. He wants us to take care of all those in need because He loves them so dearly. He even went as far as comparing Himself to them by saying this, *"Assuredly, I say to you, inasmuch as you did it to one of the least of these My brethren, you did it to Me."*- Matthew 25:40.

Volunteer in your Community

We can serve people in our neighborhood by volunteering in food banks, youth clubs/groups, hospital and prison ministries, and other platforms created by the church to reach the underprivileged, destitute, and the sick.

"And let us not grow weary of doing good, for in due season we will reap, if we do not give up." - Galatians 6:9

We can serve in any of these areas by donating cash and other basic things like clothing. It can be a few dollars or used clothes that are still in good shape. We should wash and iron them before donating them. In doing these little acts of love and service, we are touching the lives of people and that of God.

Bear the Burdens of Others

Bear one another's burdens, and so fulfill the law of Christ. - Galatians 6:2. There are so many people going through depression, feeling of disappointment, mourning, heartbreak, and many other emotional pains. They need our encouragement and our shoulder to lean unto. We need to be there for them and never make them feel lonely or abandoned.

According to Galatians 6:2, if we show people who are at their low state love, care, and support, we are fulfilling the law of Christ which says we should love our neighbors as ourselves. Being there for those experiencing emotional pain can be by visiting them, sending encouraging words via text messages or social media, calling to know how they are doing, helping them do their dishes, laundry, and other household chores.

Be Kind to Others

We can serve others by doing little acts of kindness like giving a warm hug, showing empathy, lending a listening ear, complementing, forgiving, and so on. God will be pleased with us when we do these things unto others.

Be kind to one another, tenderhearted, forgiving one another, as God in Christ forgave you. - Ephesians 4:32.

CHAPTER EIGHT

Dealing with The Unsaved While Serving

The focus of the ministry of Jesus is to the unsaved. Jesus said in Matthew 15:24 that He came, not for the saved but for the lost sheep of Israel. What this means is that Jesus came solely for unbelievers that they might be saved from sin and receive salvation and eternal life.

The love of Jesus for sinners is demonstrated in the story of lost sheep where the Shepherd (Jesus) left the 99 sheep to look for the one sheep that was lost.

The 99 sheep Jesus left behind are saved. Leaving them does not mean Jesus cares less for them. The saved have been with Jesus, learned from Him, and drank from the cup of His wisdom. They have also received power and authority to protect themselves and deal with the Kingdom of darkness and its evil forces.

The lost sheep (sinner), on the other hand, is vulnerable and an easy target for the weak ones of this world. It can be attacked and devoured easily by a lion (1 Peter 5:8.) He can also wander and fall into a ditch, break some bones, and remain there until death snatches it away. Jesus understands these dangers the lost sheep is susceptible to.

That is why He went after it to deliver it and bring it back to the fold to be amongst others.

We are to follow the example of Jesus. We must know that we have not come to serve only the saved church but to serve unbelievers. We serve them by first taking the Gospel of Christ to them. We must preach salvation to them and tell them about the love of Christ. We must ensure that we save them from the devil who is roaming around the world seeking for the vulnerable to devour.

Our service to the unsaved falls into our outreach ministry as believers. It is a commission we must fulfill because Jesus has commanded us to serve in this area (Matthew 28:18-20, Mark 16:15-18.)

How to serve the unsaved

Preach to them

The best way to reach out to the unsaved when serving is to share the Gospel of Jesus Christ with them. We should tell them about the love of Christ and how He came to die for their sins so that they may receive forgiveness of all their sins and receive eternal life. We must do this in love and not in condemnation. Jesus said, *"Go into all the world and preach the gospel to every creature."* - Mark 16:15.

Baptize them

After they have accepted Jesus Christ as their Lord and Savior and become born-again, we must ensure they go through water baptism as Jesus has commanded in Mark 16:16 *"He who believes and is baptized will be saved."* Baptism signifies the entrance into a New Covenant of Christ by dying and resurrecting with Him.

Teach them

Teaching about the Kingdom of God and the love of Christ is another way we can serve unbelievers. Jesus said we should go out to the unsaved to *"teach them to observe all things that I have commanded you"* - Matthew 28:20. We are expected to let them know about the new faith we are introducing to them and the benefits, like peace, joy, divine health, blessings, etc., they will enjoy if they forsake their sinful ways and begin to walk in holiness.

CHAPTER NINE

What Are the Blessings of Serving God?

When we serve well and give our best as good employees in our places of work. We often get rewarded with an award of the best employee, a promotion, or a raise in salary. These are ways our earthly men cherish our services and appreciate them.

It pays to serve God and He is faithful in rewarding those who serve Him diligently.

"For he who comes to God must believe that He is, and that He is a rewarder of those who diligently seek Him." Hebrews 11:6

Serving God may be demanding but rewarding. The rewards are abundant, and they are both spiritual and physical blessings. Here are some blessings we enjoy when we serve God.

We Discover and Build our Gifts

Many people have discovered their gifts in the place of serving God. Those who hitherto did not have any idea of what their calling is, or what gift of the Spirit is in them discovered themselves when serving God. God has emboldened shy people to stand in front of a congregation and teach the Word. Others have discovered their gifts of healing, prophecy, words of knowledge, words of wisdom, and others.

It does not end at discovering these gifts alone. Because of the constant use of these gifts in serving God in and outside the church, many believers have learned much more about these gifts and how best to serve with them.

We Experience Joy and Peace for Obeying God

God wants us to serve. He has called us to serve Him. *"As each one has received a gift, minister it to one another, as good stewards of the manifold grace of God."* - 1 Peter 4:10.

Serving allows us to experience the joy and peace that comes from obedience. When we obey God by serving Him, our hearts will be free from guilt caused by disobedience. We will enjoy the joy and the peace of God always.

We Surround Ourselves With other Christians

When we serve God, especially in the church, we will always be around other Christians who are passionate about serving God and doing His will.

There are huge benefits in constantly being around believers. The Bible says that iron sharpens iron (Proverbs 27:17.) That means that we can never be blunt in the knowledge of the Word of God and His service. They will always motivate and encourage us when we experience burnout or discouragement.

Serving also surrounds us with other Christians who can help us follow Jesus. They can share their revelation and experience about their personal walk with Christ and we can learn a lot from them. We are never isolated or lonely when we serve God.

We build Our Faith

Our faith is strengthened when we experience the blessings of serving. e.g., miracles of healing, deliverance, etc. When we get a firsthand experience of the power of God when serving, our faith will become stronger. Serving gives us the privilege to see the move of God and the workings of miracles, signs, and wonders.

We Become Like Jesus

The more we serve, the more we become like Jesus. We will begin to see people the same way Jesus saw them when He was still on earth. We will become humble like Jesus like he demonstrated when He washed the feet of His disciples (John 13:1–17).

We will be filled with compassion. We can see from many instances in the Bible that Jesus was always moved by compassion before healing the sick or performing in the form of a miracle (Luke 7:13, Matthew 15:32).

CHAPTER TEN

Serving God in an Online Church

What does it mean to serve online?

The world is evolving, and so is the way we do things. The church of God is not of this world but in this world. So new trends such as technological advancement will affect it.

Many companies and organizations, including the church, have both online and offline presence. The global pandemic, which led to the shutdown of churches all over the world, served as a reminder of how important having a virtual church is.

Many churches that already have websites and social media accounts like YouTube found it easy to transition to online and continue their services, while others had to rush online to continue serving God and people.

Going online means every activity conducted in the physical church will be replicated online, and people will be needed to make it happen. That is what serving online means, doing the work of the Kingdom of God online just as in the four corners of the physical church. There is only a change of location, but the principle and blessings of serving God remain constant.

How do you serve online?

Having IT knowledge is important, but there are other areas we can serve effectively without being a tech whiz. Anyone who can use a smartphone or PC and social media will serve God and the Church effectively.

There are many areas to choose from and serve. Every service rendered offline is still needed online. Then there are also areas where specific skills are required. We can serve in an online church as:

- Music Ministers(singing and musical instruments)
- Teachers
- Prayer Partners
- Greeters
- First Timers and Follow-up Ministers
- Scriptures and Sermon's Slides Designer
- Counselors
- Graphic Designers
- Social Media Managers

- Content Creators
- Sound/Audio Engineers
- Photographers
- Online Adverts Managers
- Website Developers
- Financial Accountant
- Volunteers Screening and Training Minister

The Benefits of Serving Online.

The benefits of serving online are pretty much the same as in the local church. Here are some other benefits we enjoy when we serve online.

Reaching More People

Serving online allows us to minister to a larger crowd all over the world. With the help of technology, fulfilling the great commission of Jesus, which says we should preach the gospel to all nations becomes more achievable and easier (Matthew 28:16-20).

We can serve millions of people within a few hours right from where we are, be sources of blessings unto them and bring glory to God.

Finding Purpose

Many people have found meaning and purpose in serving God online. Certain people in the church wanted to serve in the local church but could not fit in because they felt there was no place for their skills and talents. But, with churches operating majorly online now, these set of believers now have the platform to express themselves using their online skills.

Being a Change Agent

The global pandemic has brought a change to world systems and how they operate. The church is not exempted. Being a part of those driving this change through service comes with a good feeling that we are obeying God, providing solutions, and touching lives.

God Will Increase You.

The parable of the talents in Matthew 25:14-30 illustrates what happens when we serve God with the gifts He has granted us. He will give us more gifts and grace to serve at a higher capacity. If we are diligent in our service, the Word of God guarantees promotion and more opportunities.

Seest thou a man diligent in his business? He shall stand before kings: he shall not stand before mean men. - Proverbs 22:29 KJV

How to Serve Effectively Online

Here are some of the things to note when serving online.

Know that Serving Virtually and On-site are The Same.

Let your approach and attitude while serving online be the same as when you are in the physical church. Do not be like the Pharisees who did eye service and seek to please men and not God.
When we understand that our service is to God and his people, irrespective of where we are, we will serve diligently because God is everywhere.

Remove Distractions.

Ensure that you eliminate everything that can cause distractions during service. We might be tempted to do other things while serving online because we are sometimes in the comfort of our bedroom. So, because no one is there with us, we can rush while serving, eat and drink or dash into the laundry room to put some dirty clothes into the washer.

That is wrong. No matter where we are, we are in the presence of the Lord. We should take care of everything before coming to serve. Switch off your TV, stay in a quiet room and do the work of your father in heaven.

Update and Upgrade Your Skills.

We need to yearn to give God our best always. God loves it when we offer quality service to Him. God accepted the sacrifice of Abel because he gave God the fat portions from some of the firstborn of his flock (Genesis 4:4.)

To be able to serve well, we must update our skills by buying courses, reading books, doing research online, attending workshops, webinars, etc. We need to open our eyes and ears to what is trending and open our minds to find ways to incorporate these trends into our service online.

We must be creative in our service to God and give people the best experience of God so that they will come back for more again and again.

Take Your Health Seriously.

Serving online sometimes involves spending long hours sitting in front of a computer screen. That can have some health implications like itchy eyes, weight issues, low energy, etc. It is advisable to find time to exercise and take a break from the screen. Take a long walk to refresh your mind and regain energy.

CHAPTER ELEVEN

What Are the Types of Ministries?

And He Himself gave some to be apostles, some prophets, some evangelists, and some pastors and teachers, for the equipping of the saints for the work of ministry, for the edifying of the body of Christ, - Ephesians 4:11–12

According to the Bible, there are five types of ministries. They are the apostolic ministry, the prophetic ministry, the teaching ministry, the evangelistic ministry, and the pastoral ministry.

These ministries are also known as the five-fold ministry. I Corinthians 12:28 also confirmed these ministries.

You must be called into one of these ministries by God. You cannot choose to be in any ministry like you choose a career. You must meet some criteria first. They are: being born again, filled with the Holy Spirit, and then called to serve. However, a minister can have a career outside his ministry, even though some are called to full-time ministries.

As believers, we are all called to serve God and the church, but not everyone is called into ministry. Just as we cannot wake up one morning and call ourselves medical doctors without the necessary training, we cannot say we are prophets or evangelists without being called into that ministry by God.

All ministries work together for the good of the church, but they have particular roles to play. Here are some of the roles that ministers called into the five-fold ministry play in the Body of Christ.

The Apostle

The apostle lays the foundations of local churches and ensures that they grow into maturity. He has authority over those churches, overseeing the activities according to the principles of the Bible, nurturing the members with the right knowledge, until they come to the fullness of Christ.

"Even though I may not be an apostle to others, surely I am to you! For you are the seal of my apostleship in the Lord." - 1 Corinthians 9:2.

Since planting local churches is a key role of an apostle, he will likely be on the move most times to encourage the church and supervise it. Apostles disciple people with the truth in the doctrine of Christ and the Kingdom of God.

The Prophet

Prophets reveal the heart of God to the people. They guide the church, give revelations and interpret them, and give clear instructions. They have revelations of hidden things in the future. They have the foresight of things to come, and prepare the church for it, by giving clear instructions and guides, based on the Word of God.

They often hear directly from God. Sometimes, God drops a word in their hearts for the church. Irrespective of the method through which God speaks to His prophets, whatever they say must be in line with the written Word of God in the Bible. That is the test of a true prophet.

A prophet is not a fortune teller. He only speaks what God reveals to him, and he operates under the influence of the Holy Spirit.

The Evangelist

The primary goal of an evangelist is to win souls for Christ. They carry a burden in their hearts for the unsaved. They go about preaching the Gospel of salvation, converting souls, and baptizing them.

They introduce these new converts to the local church and go out to bring more. The mission field is their primary office. Signs and wonders follow them to confirm their words and to move unbelievers to acknowledge the authority in the name of Jesus and to make it easier for them to accept Christ.

Although Jesus Christ has given the mandate to win souls to all believers, an evangelist has a special calling in this regard and has a special anointing. Just as John the

Baptist, the central theme of their sermon is repentance and the second coming of Christ.

The Pastor

This is the most popular ministry of the five. The pastor is the head of the church and shepherd of the sheep. His goal is to nature the sheep, protect them and meet their needs.

He is concerned with the spiritual, emotional, and social well-being of his sheep, and will do all it takes for them to be comfortable. Sometimes, the pastor oversees the other ministries, serving as a mediator when there is conflict.

The pastor also teaches the Word of God to his church, grooming them in the ways of the Lord and helping them develop their gifts, and putting them to use.

The Teacher

Simply put, a teacher teaches. His ministry seeks to reveal the mysteries in the Bible to the church. He shares revelations in the Word of God. The teacher answers difficult questions about the Bible and gives clarifications where necessary.

His goal is to feed the church with the undiluted Word of God to the point of maturity. They have insights into God's Word and the gift of breaking complex and difficult areas of the Bible down for easy understanding.

These five-fold ministries are to function as one to serve the church and God. They are to use their gifts not to seek glory for themselves but to worship God and build His church.

CHAPTER TWELVE

Being Comfortable with Your Ministry Calling

We need each other, and we are all working towards one goal, which is to do the will of God and serve His church. No ministry is greater than the other, they are interdependent and function to fulfill the same purpose.

No matter how insignificant your service might look, it is recorded in heaven as good works. God does not look at the size of a ministry, He is interested in our hearts and attitude towards what He has given to us to do.

Diligence in little means promotion and blessings, just as we see in the talents' parable in Matthew 25:14-30. If you are faithful in little, you will be trusted with bigger things. The size of your ministry does not matter. Being on the center stage or limelight does not matter. What matters is being productive with the little given to us. Gratitude for our calling will remove jealousy and envy from our hearts and make us focus on the work placed in our hands.

Do not bury your gift because you feel it is of less value. By doing that, you are wasting the investment of God in your life. You are also denying the church the benefits of your service. Most importantly, you are blocking your way to greatness and growth in ministry because only a faithful servant receives a reward.

Always remember that when you are faithful in your calling, God will bless and reward your labor of love in His vineyard.

Here are three things we should put to practice to be comfortable with our calling.

Reaffirm your call

You are where you are supposed to be. God called you to serve in your ministry. He has a purpose for you. Anytime you feel frustrated and doubtful of your ministry calling, remind yourself why you are there and who called you to be there.

Accept who you are

You are fearfully and wonderfully made (Psalm 139:14.) Accept your uniqueness and use it to your advantage. Cultivate your gifts and maximize your potential in your ministry. Your uniqueness is an advantage, not a disadvantage. Focus less on what others are doing in their ministries and focus more on what you have and what you can do for God.

Be confident in your place of ministry.

Be confident that God called you and He is with you. You are not alone. He has empowered you to serve effectively. His presence is there with you in the place of your ministry, and He will not abandon you.

CHAPTER THIRTEEN

Avoiding Burnout in Ministry

Spiritual burnout is a problem many church leaders are facing today. The church is a beehive of activities. When we are called to ministry whether full-time or part-time, we know that we are dedicating all our lives to serve God and His people. Working for God can be demanding and along the way we will be physically, emotionally, and spiritually drained. When we feel this way, we are experiencing burnout.

Honestly, not experiencing burnout is almost impossible when we are in ministry, but what is possible is that we can manage it or better still avoid it.

To successfully manage burnout in ministry, there are necessary steps we need to take. We take some lessons from the lives of great men in the Old Testament who experienced burnout, and who managed it well and ended up serving God and His people exceptionally. They are Moses and Prophet Elijah.

Moses suffered physical burnout after sitting down from morning till night judging matters and handling the affairs of about two million people every day (Exodus 18:13). Elijah on the other experienced spiritual and emotional burnout after expending so much spiritual and physical energy when performing miracles, praying, and other spiritual affairs. He was so much drained to the point that he wished death upon himself (1 Kings 19:4).

Let us learn some principles these great men applied to manage burnout, and how we can apply them to avoid it.

Moses

In the case of Moses, he was lucky enough to have his father-in-law Jethro around to mentor him and give him sound counsel on how to avoid burnout, after seeing how he spent so much time and energy working from dawn till twilight. Here are the three principles Jethro shared with Moses to make him efficient, productive, and healthy.

Teach others

"And you shall teach them the statutes and the laws, and show them the way in which they must walk and the work they must do." - Exodus 18:20.

One of the reasons Moses took upon himself the huge responsibility of judging the people is that he was the only person that understood the laws of God. He alone knows how to resolve conflicts, judge, punish, reward, etc., the people based on the law of God. Jethro advised him to teach people about these laws so that they too can proceed over cases and disputes.

To avoid burnout, we must train people and teach them the ways of the Lord, so that they can help us with some tasks while we rest or take care of other affairs.

Choose Competent People

"Moreover you shall select from all the people able men, such as fear God, men of truth, hating covetousness; and place such over them to be rulers of thousands, rulers of hundreds, rulers of fifties, and rulers of tens." - Exodus 18:21

It is important to delegate and outsource tasks to competent people who can get the job done.
When selecting people who will help us with our ministry tasks, we must ensure they are God-fearing, spirit-filled,

faithful, and competent. The men Moses selected helped him to do some of the jobs not because they were Israelites alone but because they were skillful and able to deliver.

If this is done right, we will not experience burnout.

Handle only the Most Difficult Tasks

"Then it will be that every great matter they shall bring to you, but every small matter they themselves shall judge. So it will be easier for you, for they will bear the burden with you." - Exodus 18:22

Jethro advised Moses to only handle the most difficult tasks the people he had chosen cannot deal with. This strategy has two advantages. The first benefit is Moses will have enough time, physical and mental strength to deal with such difficult tasks. The second benefit is that he will be focused on these difficult tasks and it will be easy to come up with solutions.

Handling only the most difficult tasks will not only conserve our energy and save our time, but it will also help us to be efficient and productive.

Elijah

Elijah's burnout was so intense that he wanted his life to end. This is the same man who called down fire from heaven, outran chariots, and did so many other mighty miracles. However, when he was threatened by just one woman, Jezebel, he became afraid and depressed. However, God helped Elijah to overcome the phase of emotional burnout he experienced, and we can derive some lessons that we can apply to our ministries today. They are rest and nourishment 1 Kings 19:5-8.

Nourishment

"...suddenly an angel touched him, and said to him, "Arise and eat." - 1 Kings 19:5

God miraculously provided baked cake and a jar of water, which Elijah ate and drank from. God knew how exhausted he was, and he understood exactly what he needed to regain his strength.

Many times, we are caught up in a lot of activities in ministry that we hardly find time to eat. Sometimes, we even forget that we have not eaten. This can cause burnout. We need a healthy body to serve God, and food and water are essential. Only a healthy person can serve effectively. We must find time to eat healthy foods, not junk and soda, but fresh foods like fruits and other well-cooked meals. This will boost our energy and avoid burnout.

Rest

"Then as he lay and slept under a broom tree" - 1 Kings 19:5

After each meal, the angel God sent to Elijah told him to sleep. This happened twice (1 Kings 19:5-6). The place of rest cannot be overemphasized in service. Even God rested on the seventh day after six busy days of creation.

As servants of God, we often find ourselves on the move. We juggle work, family, church services, and many other activities. We end up working morning, noon, and night, and hardly have time to sleep properly. We end up stressed and tired, weak, overwhelmed, and discouraged.

God wants us to rest. God created day and night before He created man because He knew that he would need to sleep. Psalm 127:2 says, *"God gives His beloved sleep."*

To avoid burnout in ministry, we must prioritize rest and sleep. Short naps in the daytime and proper sleep at night and we will always be energized to serve.

CHAPTER FOURTEEN

Setting Ministry Boundaries

Setting boundaries in ministry is important for any minister that wants to go far.
Here are three key areas where boundaries must be set in a ministry.

Access and Time

When you are a ministry leader, you frequently have people knocking on your door and calling your phone. Attending to them is what you are meant to do. It is a part of your service to them and what God has called you to do but set boundaries so that you will not burnout.

Yes, you are called to serve everyone but ensure that you set some boundaries, so that you can have time for your personal life and family. Have time for visitation, counseling, and other obligations you have.

One way to set boundaries to access is, for instance, not attending to church affairs in your home. Ensuring that 100% of your time at home is dedicated to yourself, kids, and spouse. Having enough time for yourself is still to the advantage of the people you serve and your ministry because you will have the opportunity to rest, refresh and regain strength.

As a minister, you need time to grow so that you will be able to serve better and help the church grow, but this cannot be possible if you are always serving or attending to the people.

Put structures in place so that the ministry can still run successfully without you being around. Do not make your ministry all about yourself. Train men and women to serve and assist you.
Create a schedule to help the people you serve know when you are available and not.

Dealing with the Opposite Gender

This issue has raised a lot of interest and has caused scandals around many ministries and their leaders. We must understand that we are first humans before we are ministers. We have blood running through our veins. We have emotions and feelings, and it remains like that irrespective of how powerful our anointing to serve is.

Ministry leaders must be strict in this regard. The boundary must be strict, and tight as much as possible because many have fallen in this aspect. We must be careful when dealing with the opposite sex. This is not about being canal or fleshly; it is about putting the body under subjection and guarding the heart.

As a male minister, ensure your wife is always with you, especially when you have a one-on-one meeting, counseling session, etc., with a woman. Women in ministry should do the same.
When we notice that we are getting too close or comfortable with the opposite sex in such a way we know

that it could lead to sin, we must cut any relationship between us with such a person, assign someone else to attend to the needs of such person, preferably someone of the same gender.

Avoid private meetings. If there is a need for secrecy, meet in the office but leave the door open, or have your spouse around. Do what it takes to not fall into sin. The Bible gives direct instruction concerning sexual sin. It says we should flee. Not walk away, not pray but run for dear life. 2 Timothy 2:22, 1 Thessalonians 5:22.

Activities

All things are lawful for me, but not all things are helpful; all things are lawful for me, but not all things edify - 1 Corinthians 10:23
As ministers, we must set boundaries on the places we go and the things we do. We should erase the mindset that we can go anywhere or do anything we want because we are filled with the Holy Spirit.

The apostle Paul said all things are lawful to him, but all things are not permissible. We must learn from this and ensure that we put our activities to check for the sake of the people we serve.

As a minister, if you had issues with sexual sins and lust of the flesh and struggled with pornography before being saved, you have no business visiting brothels, strip clubs, etc., to evangelize. Let others do it. Stay away from alcohol if you were once an alcoholic. Be disciplined and strict about parties and other functions you attend.

We must also place a boundary on the kind of movies we watch and the kind of music we listen to, for our benefit and the church.

CHAPTER FIFTEEN

Balancing Ministry and Family

The devil loves to attack the family of those dedicated to service in the church, especially leaders of the ministry. The strategy is simple; if you hit the shepherd, the flock will scatter (Zechariah 13:7, Matthew 26:31).

Satan is fully aware of this, that is why he targets the families of ministry leaders. He attacks their family, spouse or children. It is almost common to see pastors' kids and the children of dedicated workers in church wayward. It is really something that has almost become a stereotype.

This began in the Old Testament. A typical example is Eli, whose children Hophni and Phinehas treated the sacrifices offered to God with contempt and committed adultery with the women who served at the temple. The striking thing about this story is that Eli was so caught up in his service as the high priest that he did not know how wayward his children had become. In fact, he heard about their escapades from outsiders (1 Samuel 2:12-36.) To cut the long story short, Eli's two sons died on the same day as a consequence of their sins.

The problem here is that most people serving in ministry are so much deep into service that they give little or no attention to their children and spouses. They are always in the church handling Bible study or Sunday school, or they are outside in the field spreading the Gospel of Christ. When they get home, it is already late, the kids are asleep, and they are exhausted.
Also, they spend less time with their families, and they do not have a family altar because they are off to church early in the morning.

The accumulation of all these can affect the family in many ways if not checked. There is a need to create a balance between family and ministry. Ministers need to know that a failed family is as good as a failed ministry. This is evident in the life of Eli the High Priest.

How then can you balance ministry and family?

Deal with the Messiah-Complex

An average leader has this feeling that they have to be the one to save the day, make huge sacrifices, do the heavy lifting, and lay down their entire life (time, energy, money, resources) for a course. Ministry leaders are also guilty of this complex. They are almost in every part of the ministry. They do counseling, teaching, being part of the teams that organize programs in and out of the church, and so on. The resultant effect of this is they become physically and emotionally drained and have no more energy left for the family.

The best way to deal with this is to give up the mindset that they have to always make sacrifices even when not necessary.

Give up Perfectionism

As ministry leaders, we might feel that no one can do it like I do or something will go wrong if I am not there. That is far from the truth. God has blessed many people with excellent Spirit and the wisdom of God to work for Him. If we give them the chance God will work through them and we will be amazed at how well they will do the job. It is God who equips and empowers man to serve.

Build a Reliable Team

Our Lord Jesus Christ, the greatest master who ever lived on earth, had to build a team to help Him do the work of the kingdom. The ministry of Jesus should be our template. Jesus constantly taught His team members (disciples), empowered them, and then gave them work to do so that he can focus on other things. Build a reliable team and delegate tasks to them.

Create Time for Family

We should be intentional about creating time for family. Try to pick kids up from school twice or three times a week, make plans for family picnics, and have holidays for family bonding. Men should take their wives out for dinner or see a movie. Women in ministry should also find ways to spend quality time with their husbands.

Supporting your Spouse who is in Ministry

Marriage is a partnership - a partnership in building a home and family, building business, life, and ministry with your spouse. When you agree to marry a person, you are saying that you have decided to support your spouse to achieve their goals, fulfill their dreams, and accomplish their purpose. This decision applies to the ministry. When God calls your spouse into ministry, you need to support them in every way you can.

Also, you need to know that when He calls your spouse to do His work, He is also calling you to support. You are the biggest supporter of your spouse's calling or ministry, not the church members or Personal Assistance. It does not matter whether it is the man or woman God has called into ministry; it is essential to find ways to help lessen the burden and be a support system.

Supporting your spouse in ministry reinforces that a marriage is a covenant, so rather than neglecting the other when entering into ministry, they can travel in parallel as man and wife working for God. Marriage and ministry is a duet, not a solo. There are many ways you can be a pillar of strength and grease in the wheels of your spouse's ministry.

Learn to Make sacrifices

There will be times when your spouse will spend long hours in their office counseling people and meeting their needs while you sit and wait. There will also be times when your spouse will be busy answering phone calls and replying to emails on ministry matters instead of spending quality time with you and your family. Other times they might travel out of the city instead of vacationing with you and the children.

These are some of the moments when your spouse needs your support the most, even though it might be difficult.

Know that when you sacrifice your time, energy, and resources for your spouse in ministry, you are not only helping them, but you are also doing the Lord's work, and He will reward you.

Review Sermons

If your spouse is a pastor, teacher, preacher, or in any area of ministry which requires them to prepare sermons or the Word and speak to people, you can support them by helping in reviewing their notes.

Read their sermons, edit, proofread, and make suggestions where necessary. Always let your spouse feel they can use you as a sounding board rather than thinking alone.

Doing this shows you are interested in their calling and are willing to help them serve God.

Do Dress Rehearsals

Be the first audience of your spouse. Be the first ears to hear what they want to say, be the first eyes to see what they want to do and be the first hands to applaud them.

If your spouse's ministry is evangelism or counseling, for example, before they go out to minister to someone, let them minister to you first.

Sit down attentively and listen to all they have to say. Then, encourage your spouse by stating how well they did and work together in areas that need improvement.

Doing this will boost your spouse's confidence and help them give their best in service to God.

Create a Schedule

One of the ways you can help your spouse in ministry as a man or woman is by creating a schedule that will help your spouse work effectively. Working effectively in ministry means balancing ministry with family time and me-time. Work with your partner to create a schedule that would help them work for God, spend time with you and the kids, and have time to rest to reduce stress or restore energy.

Encourage Your Spouse

Your words are powerful; use them to uplift and encourage your spouse as they do work for God. Tell them how wonderfully well they are performing in their ministry. Let them know how powerful their sermons are and how they are transforming lives, including yours.

Be your spouse's feedback mechanism. They always need to hear from you. What others say about them has less importance compared to when they hear them from you.

Pray for them and bless them.

CHAPTER SIXTEEN

Managing Ministry Conflict

I planted, Apollos watered, but God gave the increase. - 1 Corinthians 3:7.
That statement was made by the Apostle Paul when there was conflict among the Christians in Corinth over who was greater between Paul and Apollos.

Arguments and conflicts of this nature still happen in ministries today. Paul stressed that the cause of this kind of behavior is carnality. *"For when one says, "I am of Paul," and another, "I am of Apollos," are you not carnal?"* - 1 Corinthians 3:4.

Here are some mindsets that lead to conflicts in ministry.

Not understanding the concept of service.

Conflict can easily erupt when people serving do not understand what it means to serve in a ministry in the first place. What does service mean? Who are we serving? Why are we serving?

If we cannot answer these questions correctly, then we will not be able to serve correctly. When the purpose of a thing is not known, abuse is inevitable.

The Christians in Corinth were caught up in this web, and the apostle Paul called them canal.

Pride

When you begin to feel too important. When you think so highly of yourself, and you feel you are too big to take instructions and directives, especially when you are serving under a ministry leader, the conflict will happen.

That is caused by pride, which caused the great war in heaven between the forces of Lucifer (now Satan) and the army of God. Satan felt he deserved to rule because he was created an archangel and given singing abilities (Isaiah 14:13). He gathered himself loyalists, and he rebelled against God. This action led to his eviction from heaven and a judgment of eternal perdition in hell (Revelation 12:7-11).

Envy

It comes from the feeling that others are doing better than us in ministry. Maybe because people prefer to join the Sunday school class of a particular brother or sister in the church because of how such a person teaches, you begin to nurse some bitter thoughts towards such a fellow.

Where there is envy, there is conflict. *"For where there are envy, strife, and divisions among you, are you not carnal and behaving like mere men?."* - 1 Corinthians 3:3.

It could also be that we are envious of the gift of others. We might feel jealous of a teacher or preacher who mounts the podium to preach and gets a standing ovation, while we serve as counselors quietly behind closed doors, or clean the church on Saturdays when no one sees us serving.

Not feeling appreciated

When we feel we are not celebrated or appreciated enough for our service in a ministry, this can lead to a roller-coaster of feelings that can cause conflict in a ministry. Another problem here is when we feel others are appreciated more than us, even when we always give our all to serve. Some can also feel this way when they are not paid for their service or given gifts for a job well done.

Feeling overburdened

There will come a time when we feel overburdened or overused by the ministry we serve, especially when we are diligent, faithful, and trustworthy. We might feel like the weight of the ministry is placed on our shoulders, and we are bearing it alone. It becomes worse when we see others doing little or nothing at all.

We begin to experience burnout and the feeling of frustration, which in turn can lead to anger and outburst towards the leader of the ministry or others serving with us.

How To Manage Conflicts in Ministry

Now that we know what might be responsible for conflicts. Let us see some ways we can manage them.

Focus on Jesus

Fix your gaze on Jesus alone and know within your heart that your services are unto Him alone. *Looking on to Jesus the author and finisher of our faith* - Hebrews 12:2.

We are not to serve the leader of the ministry; the team leads in such a way that we are pleasing them or seeking favor. Our service is a form of worship to our God, who sees all and knows the thoughts and intentions of our hearts.

God is a Rewarder

But without faith, it is impossible to please Him, for he who comes to God must believe that He is, and that He is a rewarder of those who diligently seek Him. - Hebrews 11:6

The blessings that come from God supersedes any form of a standing ovation, gifts, or cash any man would give. The blessings of the Lord make one rich and adds no sorrow with it (Proverbs 10:22.)

We are one Body in Christ.

So we, being many, are one body in Christ, and individually members of one another. - Romans 12:5.

We are one body in Christ, and we all need each other to function properly. No matter how insignificant we feel certain gifts are, the ministry will not function well without them. No gift is greater than the other. The absence of one will cause a vacuum and make ministry dysfunctional.

Desire the best gifts

But earnestly desire the best gifts. And yet I show you a more excellent way. - 1 Corinthians 12:31

The Bible says we should covet good gifts, not envy them. To covet based on that Biblical context is to crave or desire. To envy is to be bitter or become angry about the progress or shine of another person.

When we are ruled by envy, there are bound to be conflicts in the ministry we serve. Envy can lead to an argument, and it can blow up to become full-blown verbal or physical abuse if not checked.

To whom much is given, much is expected.

He who is faithful in what is least is faithful also in much - Luke 16:10

The more you prove to be diligent and faithful in serving, God will entrust more responsibility to you. God has prepared you as a vessel of honor for His use (2 Timothy 2:20-21.) When you feel tired and overburdened, seek out time to rest and recharge. Ask God for strength and for helpers who will join you to serve Him.

Be Humble

No matter how well God is using you. No matter how good you think you are, always wear humility like a cloth. Stay humble. Be intentional about it. When people begin to sing your praises and praise you, do not let it get into your head. Give God the glory. Be humble, and God will lift you by Himself. God hates pride (James 4:6).

CHAPTER SEVENTEEN

Scriptures on Serving in Ministry

But in a great house there are not only vessels of gold and silver, but also of wood and clay, some for honor and some for dishonor. Therefore, if anyone cleanses himself from the latter, he will be a vessel for honor, sanctified and useful for the Master, prepared for every good work.
2 Timothy 2:20-21

And whatever you do, do it heartily, as to the Lord and not to men.
Colossians 3:23

As each one has received a gift, minister it to one another, as good stewards of the manifold grace of God. If anyone speaks, let him speak as the oracles of God. If anyone ministers, let him do it as with the ability which God supplies, that in all things God may be glorified through

Jesus Christ, to whom belong the glory and the dominion forever and ever. Amen.
1 Peter 4:10-11

Then the King will say to those on His right hand, 'Come, you blessed of My Father, inherit the kingdom prepared for you from the foundation of the world: for I was hungry and you gave Me food; I was thirsty and you gave Me drink; I was a stranger and you took Me in; I was naked and you clothed Me; I was sick and you visited Me; I was in prison and you came to Me.' **Matthew 25:34-36**

Knowing that from the Lord you will receive the reward of the inheritance; for you serve the Lord Christ. **Colossians 3:24**

You shall walk after the Lord your God and fear Him, and keep His commandments and obey His voice; you shall serve Him and hold fast to Him. **Deuteronomy 13:4**

For we are His workmanship, created in Christ Jesus for good works, which God prepared beforehand that we should walk in them. **Ephesians 2:10**

And be kind to one another, tenderhearted, forgiving one another, even as God in Christ forgave you. **Ephesians 4:32**

Submitting to one another in the fear of God. **Ephesians 5:21**

All Scripture is given by inspiration of God, and is profitable for doctrine, for reproof, for correction, for instruction in righteousness, that the man of God may be complete, thoroughly equipped for every good work. **2 Timothy 3:16-17**

But you shall receive power when the Holy Spirit has come upon you; and you shall be witnesses to Me in Jerusalem, and in all Judea and Samaria, and to the end of the earth.
Acts 1:8

I have shown you in every way, by laboring like this, that you must support the weak. And remember the words of the Lord Jesus, that He said, 'It is more blessed to give than to receive.'
Acts 20:35

And whatever you do in word or deed, do all in the name of the Lord Jesus, giving thanks to God the Father through Him. **Colossians 3:17**

Therefore, my beloved brothers, be steadfast, immovable, always abounding in the work of the Lord, knowing that in the Lord your labor is not in vain. **1 Corinthians 15:58**

Let all that you do be done with love. **1 Corinthians 16:14**

For though I am free from all, I have made myself a servant to all, that I might win more. **1 Corinthians 9:19**

My little children let us not love in word or in tongue, but in deed and in truth. **1 John 3:18**

But as He who called you is holy, you also be holy in all your conduct, because it is written, "Be holy, for I am holy." **1 Peter 1:15-16**

As free, yet not using liberty as a cloak for vice, but as bondservants of God. **1 Peter 2:16**

That he no longer should live the rest of his time in the flesh for the lusts of men, but for the will of God. **1 Peter 4:2**

Only fear the Lord, and serve Him in truth with all your heart; for consider what great things He has done for you. **1 Samuel 12:24**

For those who have served well as deacons obtain for themselves a good standing and great boldness in the faith which is in Christ Jesus. **1 Timothy 3:13**

But you, be strong and do not let your hands be weak, for your work shall be rewarded! **2 Chronicles 15:7**

Bear one another's burdens, and so fulfill the law of Christ. **Galatians 6:2**

And let us not grow weary while doing good, for in due season we shall reap if we do not lose heart. **Galatians 6:9**

For we do not preach ourselves, but Christ Jesus the Lord, and ourselves your bondservants for Jesus' sake. **2 Corinthians 4:5**

For you, brethren, have been called to liberty; only do not use liberty as an opportunity for the flesh, but through love serve one another. For all the law is fulfilled in one word, even in this: "You shall love your neighbor as yourself." **Galatians 5:13-14**

Therefore, as we have opportunity, let us do good to all, especially to those who are of the household of faith. **Galatians 6:10**

And let us consider one another in order to stir up love and good works, not forsaking the assembling of ourselves together, as is the manner of some, but exhorting one another, and so much the more as you see the Day approaching. **Hebrews 10:24-25**

But do not forget to do good and to share, for with such sacrifices God is well pleased.
Hebrews 13:16

For God is not unjust to forget your work and labor of love which you have shown toward His name, in that you have ministered to the saints, and do minister. **Hebrews 6:10**

How much more shall the blood of Christ, who through the eternal Spirit offered Himself without spot to God, cleanse your conscience from dead works to serve the living God? **Hebrews 9:14**

If you extend your soul to the hungry And satisfy the afflicted soul, Then your light shall dawn in the darkness, And your darkness shall be as the noonday **Isaiah 58:10**

But be doers of the word, and not hearers only, deceiving yourselves. **James 1:22**

Pure and undefiled religion before God and the Father is this: to visit orphans and widows in their trouble, and to keep oneself unspotted from the world. **James 1:27**

If anyone serves Me, let him follow Me; and where I am, there My servant will be also. If anyone serves Me, him My Father will honor. **John 12:26**

If I then, your Lord and Teacher, have washed your feet, you also ought to wash one another's feet. **John 13:14**

This is my commandment, that you love one another as I have loved you. **John 15:12**

For who is greater, he who sits at the table, or he who serves? Is it not he who sits at the table? Yet I am among you as the One who serves. **Luke 22:27**

But love your enemies, do good, and lend, hoping for nothing in return; and your reward will be great, and you will be sons of the Most High. For He is kind to the unthankful and evil.
Luke 6:35

Servant in Ministry Commitment

What challenge(s) am I facing in my ministry?

How am I dealing with these challenges?

What Ministry or Ministries did God instruct me to join?

Do I believe I have been called by God to use my skill to serve in my ministry?

Am I willing to serve the church in any way?

Am I in the Ministry God wants me to be?

What are my strengths?

What ministry or ministries can I see myself adding value to?

Am I giving my best in my ministry?

How can I improve in my service/ministry?

Am I willing to continue to improve my skills, and grow in wisdom and ability to serve better?

What am I doing to improve my service in ministry?

Who is my accountability partner(s) (AP)?

Your Signature_____

Your AP_____

Your Pastor_____

www.ingramcontent.com/pod-product-compliance
Lightning Source LLC
Chambersburg PA
CBHW071832290426
44109CB00017B/1808